How One Cup of Coffee Can Help You to Succeed in Affiliate Marketing

ROBERT THIBODEAU

Robert Thibodeau

HOW ONE CUP of COFFEE CAN HELP YOU to SUCCEED in AFFILIATE MARKETING

ROBERT THIBODEAU

ISBN: 9781098785802

Disclaimer:

The contents are based on the author's personal experience and research. Your results may vary, and will be based on your individual situation and motivation. There are no guarantees concerning the level of success you may experience. Each individual's success depends on his or her background, dedication, desire and motivation.

NOTE: Some of the recommendations in this report might contain affiliate links. If you click on the link(s) and purchase such a product based on my review and/or recommendation, I will receive a commission. Whether I receive a commission or not will not have any effect on the purchase price of the product. Additionally, I am sometimes offered a complimentary product to review. My decision to promote these products is based on my own satisfaction with the products. I do not recommend crap, and any review I make will be based on my own experiences, which are not typical. You could do better, you could do worse, you could do nothing at all, and that is totally out of my control.

We make every effort to ensure that we accurately represent our products and services. There are no guarantees that your results will match examples published in this report.

Some links may change, or may not even work, for many reasons beyond the control of the author and distributors. We cannot guarantee or otherwise be responsible for what you might find when you click through to sites not under the control of the publisher of this report.

Table of Contents

How One Cup of Coffee Can Help You to Succeed in Affiliate Marketing

Coffee is a magical drink!

It helps me to wake up in the morning. It helps me to focus at work. It helps me to relax in stressful situations. It helps to network with friends. It is also a great excuse to "get away" for a bit (and have a reason to do so)!

But in addition to all of those "benefits," Coffee can also help you to succeed in your business. It can help you to grow Spiritually. It can help you to raise a better family. It can help you in so many, innumerable ways.

This series on **"How One Cup of Coffee Can…"** has been written to take a closer look at areas in your life in which you would like to see improvement. That improvement could mean more income, more appointments, greater business results or even better relationships.

When I first wrote *"How One Cup of Coffee Can Change Your World,"* I had no idea that my concept of looking at your morning cup of "Joe" would impact so many people! By looking at your morning cup of coffee, and using it as an analogy of planning your day, I had no idea it would provide the ability to help so many people at so many different levels in so many different facets of life!

—

The Beginning...

I have to give credit where credit is due.

I did not develop this idea of looking at a cup of coffee in a different light. I received it as a bit of "humor and wisdom" mixed together, back when I was a junior officer in the US Army Cavalry.

To spare you the details with all of the Army acronyms, it was Major General Taylor (who was commanding the 5th Infantry Division at Fort Polk, Louisiana) who first described "his concept" of looking at coffee in a different light. It was in an "after action briefing after a brutal "mock battle" in which he pitted two Brigade size elements against each other (with our Cavalry squadron providing recon for one of the Brigade Commanders).

Our Squadron was able to "infiltrate" the enemy side and we pinpointed almost every tank position and headquarters elements of the "enemy." So when the battle started, it was over in about two hours! It was supposed to last for up to "two days."

I was present when the General rose to speak. He said, *"Gentlemen, all I can say is, today we "**Made Coffee.**""* He then went on to explain what he meant by that saying. And his example has stuck with me from that day to this.

I used this example the rest of the time I was in the military. I used this example to train agents and office staff after I left the Army and started my own successful business. I used this example as a police officer and as a police supervisor. I've used it in ministry and I've used it in developing a highly successful online radio station.

I've shared this story numerous times and I've seen many people take (and successfully use) the concepts I am about to share with you. I have seen and heard of people using them successfully in so many different areas of life, that I've lost count.

Basic Understanding of Making Coffee

Coffee can have a variety of mixtures, strengths, condiments, temperatures, etc. But if you strip away all of the variances, you are left with needing only FOUR ELEMENTS.

1. **COFFEE.** You MUST have coffee in order to "make coffee!"
2. **Water.** You MUST have water or you will not "make coffee!"
3. **Heat.** You MUST have a source of heat or you will not "make coffee!" (You can still make "ice coffee." But even with Ice Tea, you still need to heat the water for it to be effective. So HEAT is a requirement.
4. **Container.** You need a container to effectively "make coffee."

If you have ALL FOUR of those elements, you can "make coffee." The quality of the coffee will depend on the mixture of those four things (too little water; too much coffee = bitter coffee, etc.). If you are missing even ONE of those things, you do not "have coffee." You only have "hot water" or "burned coffee grounds," etc.

The Concept of COFFEE and How to Use It

Taking the concept of "How to Make Coffee" and turning it into a viable way to train and motivate employees and leaders at all levels (and even yourself), is easy - once you understand it.

Identify whatever it is you are trying to accomplish.
Break that task down into its main components.
Combine or eliminate repetitive things.

Reduce everything into four major areas (minimum of 3 and maximum of 5).

Review your list and make sure those four areas ARE absolutely essential to your success.

Now, focus on accomplishing those four areas! If you do that, you will have "made coffee" in whatever area you are trying to accomplish!

It is also possible to break each area down into sub-categories or tasks. If you do that, you should use the same strategy as you did for the breaking down the major areas.

For example, let's say I am rolling out a new product line (doesn't matter what it is, this is only an example).

So my major areas might be:
1. Design the product
2. Purchase materials
3. Manufacture the product
4. Market the product

Let's just focus on #3 for this example of "sub-categories."

Manufacture the Product:
1. Equipment
2. Materials
3. People
4. Training

Now, notice this. In the Major categories, I have the Four Major areas I need to be successful. In the sub-category of "Manufacture the Product," I also have four areas that need to work together in order to be successful in the "overall" category of "Manufacture the Product."

If I do not have the equipment necessary to assemble the materials, I will not have "made coffee" for that category. If I have the equipment but no materials to work with, I will not have "made coffee."

If I have the equipment and the materials, but no people to do the work and assemble everything, I have no product and I did not "make coffee."

If have the equipment, the materials and the people, but they are not trained in how to use the equipment to turn the materials into the desired product, I still have not "made coffee."

But, when I have the equipment. I have the materials. I have the people. And the people know how to use the equipment to turn the materials into the product, I have "Made Coffee" for that major category!

Now, it is on to marketing and making money!

Do you see how all of this fits together?

Focus on what is necessary to be successful and all of the "other things" will fall into place, as they are more easily managed.

I use these first few pages in all of my books. It is an easy way for you to grasp the concept of "How to Make Coffee" for your particular task at hand.

Now, let's move on to the topic of our discussion for the rest of this book!

How you can succeed at Affiliate Marketing by focusing on that

ONE CUP OF COFFEE!

How One Cup of Coffee Can Help You to Succeed in Affiliate Marketing

Who is your intended end user (client)?

Who will be the perfect client that can use the product you are promoting? If the answer is "everyone," then you will sell to "no one."

If you try to market to people in order to convince them they need the product you are promoting, you will spend a lot of valuable resources (i.e. money) and a lot of time and effort in the process. The end result will be a lot of disgruntled customers that will not want anything else to do with you in the future – AND a lot of possible returns (and chargebacks) in the process.

This could be eliminated by focusing your efforts only on those who will benefit the most from the product! You will save time and money (which can be used to reach even more of your "target market") in the process.

The ability to help someone fill a need in their life or business will build your credibility! You will be able to reach out and contact them later on and they will remember how you helped them before. This will result in future income potential for you through repeat business!

Avoiding the charge backs will help you to retain the income you are earning! There is nothing more disheartening than to think you are going to be paid a certain amount on "pay-day" and find out you are not getting a check at all because so many people cancelled and requested refunds! I know – I've lived it!

If you spend just a little bit of quality time right now, in the beginning, to actually focus on "who" your target customer is (often called your avatar), you will save time and money later! Don't be too general in this area.

If you are going to market "weight loss," are you going to help women? Or men? Young? Or old? People who are just now trying to lose weight? Or those who have tried and failed over and over and over again? Are you going to focus on diet alone? Or diet and exercise? Working out at home? Or at a gym?

As you can see, there are numerous areas just in "weight loss." You can focus on several of those areas in your training. But your primary client may be a:

"35-year old female, stay at home mom, who has tried and failed several times over the last several years to lose 20 pounds. She has no time to go to the gym, so working out at home is her best option. Dieting is difficult because she is the one doing the cooking for the family."

Do you see how specific this avatar is?
You can still market your products and offers to other

people. But each product you offer will be targeted to this specific person.

This means you will not offer "water aerobics and shuffle board" as a work out option (like you would for a 70-year old person with some disability problem).

So take some time, right now, to identify who your "perfect customer" is going to be. Then move on to the next session. Doing this now will help you to focus all of your effort later in developing the offers a lot easier.

Identify Existing Products

There are several ways for you to provide products to sell to your perfect client.

Develop the products yourself. This is a way for you to design a product around your expertise. It is a way for you to create a product that is unique to your experiences and background. This is the perfect product that you can offer for your client(s).

The problem with this method of product creation is **TIME.**

You are the person identifying the need.
You are the person deciding how best to help your perfect client to fulfill that need.
You are the person who must design and develop the training.
You are the person who must design and develop the product to fulfill the training.
You are the person who must edit, rewrite and market the product.

Do you see how much **TIME** that is going to involve? Just to create ONE product?

Another option is to PURCHASE the material and resell it to your client. This method is a better option. But there is a problem here as well.

First, you must do the research to make sure the product will meet the needs of your perfect client. Second, you need to try and negotiate a price where you will be able to resell the product at a profit. Third, you will then have to market the product and hope to sell enough to make a profit.

This is important. You will not want to go on Amazon, EBay or elsewhere and purchase a book or product at retail of (for example) $15 and then try to resell it to your client for $20. What will happen to your client the next time they are on Amazon and decide to research the book you sold them? And they find out you "cheated them" on the book sale? There goes your client! And you can almost guarantee there will be "no referral" for your services!

This is why you would have to try and negotiate a lower price so that people doing the research will see they could have purchased the same book at the same price. They don't know you negotiated the lower price on your end (i.e. "wholesale")!

Another method is to use PRIVATE LABEL RIGHTS (PLR). PLR is a great way to get the information. You will do the research. You will obtain the material at a steep discount. However, your work is not done at that point!

You need to "rewrite" the material to make it your own. That means you need to take the time to go through every single page and rewrite it.

Every. Single. Page.

Why? Because I can almost guarantee you that somebody has taken the exact same PLR you just purchased and simply put their name on it and published it already. So the search engines are identifying this material as already being "out there."

That means, as you put your name on it and "publish it," it shows up as "duplicate" content. And the more people that do the same thing, the more it is picked up as duplicated content. You could end up getting "banned" from showing up in future search results!

So, you need to rewrite all **(yes – ALL)** of the material. You need to put it all into your own words with your own "voice." It needs to "sound like you wrote it."

So, the question may be, *"Why don't I just write my own material then?"* Good question.

The reason is simple. Use the PLR as an "outline" to write your own material. You don't have to create everything from scratch. Just go through each page and rearrange and rewrite the material and change the words and sentence structure.

For example, let's say the PLR paragraph is:

"The easiest way to edit PLR is to rewrite the original material into your own words. This will allow your voice to shine through. This will help to keep the search engines from flagging your material as "duplicate content" that is already published. This will also help you to understand the material being presented. You may even find there has been some outdated information in the PLR you have. This will allow you to make sure your product is current with the information you are providing to your clients."

You can rewrite that paragraph to read:

When providing information to your clients, you want to make sure you understand everything you are sharing with them. They may ask you a question and you do not want to be taken by surprise! Sometimes, you will find PLR that has outdated information. This would not reflect well on your expertise if someone finds out the "new material" you are sharing is already outdated!

The best way of covering both of these areas is to rewrite the PLR as you go through it. Just take your time and read it through. Highlight some areas that you can identify immediately as being outdated. Do some research and insert the correct information into your product. If possible, rearrange the way the information is presented.

This will help to keep the search engines from identifying your new product as "duplicate information" and possibly flagging your content. Simply update, rearrange and rewrite the material into your own words with your own "voice." This will truly make it "your product."

Notice how I covered the exact same information contained in the first paragraph, but now it is rewritten in a "different voice!" It looks different and reads different. It contains the same information though!

This is how you need to go through, page by page, and make the PLR "yours."

Another method of providing great value to your client is to use AFFILIATE MARKETING!

Affiliate Marketing is simply taking an existing authority and the product they are offering, and reselling the information to your clients. Usually, the creator will offer the product at a discount and pay you a commission for selling it to your clients. If there should be any customer service requests in the future (for example, a link is not working), the creator handles the customer service issues, not you.

This does three things for you.

One, it eliminates the need for you to create or rewrite products and materials.

Two, it establishes you as an "expert" that is able to provide clients relevant material from other established experts.

And Three, it allows you to earn an income while helping your clients.

The only requirement you will have with Affiliate Marketing is the research to make sure the information is relevant to your "perfect avatar client." It may be used by others. But it MUST be able to be used by your "perfect client."

Since this book is dedicated expressly to Affiliate Marketing, I will spend the remainder of this book diving deep into this subject.

Researching Current Affiliate Products

Once you accurately identify "who" your potential clients are, you will need to identify "why" you are the perfect person to help them. In order to do that, you must find out what others are already teaching them and determine how you will be different.

So, do your research. Go to Google and start to research what training is available to those who are experiencing the problems you are willing to help your clients overcome. You may even purchase some of the training programs from your competitors! That does not mean you "copy" what they are doing! This is for research purposes (although you may even learn a thing or two from them that you had not been aware of)!

As you research these other training programs, you will need to look at it from an analytical point of view. I usually create a spread sheet and score each area concerning each training program I am evaluating. This way, I am able to accurately evaluate each plan and compare it to the plan I would like to offer my clients.

This system may even help you to identify weaknesses in your existing training program, allowing you can make it even better.

Identify these specific areas:

Name of the Training Plan
Author / Coach Name
Website
What specific goal is being taught to the client?
What is the specific outcome being promised to the client?
What short-comings have you identified with this plan?
How long is the training program (one week; one month; 90 days; etc.)?
How difficult is the program to implement? (novice; advanced; professional)
How much does the program cost?
Is this a "one time cost" or a "recurring cost?"
Is the program all inclusive, "done for you" or are there additional upsells?
What is the most "unique" thing this program teaches that others do not?
Is there a personal touch (i.e. personal email correspondence with the person doing the training)?
Is this a product with a dedicated customer support staff to serve the client?

By making an accurate assessment of the Affiliate Programs that have already been created, you will be able to determine which one will best serve your end user – your future clients. Remember, you want to offer something that will help them to fulfill a need they have.

You want to establish a long term relationship with them. It has been proven that it costs you more money to keep finding new clients than to nurture existing clients and having them become recurring buyers. If you get a reputation for selling everything under the sun to your list, soon you will not have a list. Or, at least it will not be a "buyer list."

Affiliate Marketing is designed to help you grow your own business by marketing a product that has been created by someone else. It's that simple!

You participate in affiliate marketing everyday – and probably do not even realize it! All department stores, gas stations, grocery stores – everything – are selling products created or provided by someone else. These people sell their products to the store. The store sells the products to you. The stores are paid to do so! It is really that simple!

Just like a major chain store will evaluate products and determine if a product is a good fit for their store, you must also evaluate products to see if they will fit with your personality and goals as well. If something does not fit with what your goals are, you do not have to become an affiliate!

But if something does match up with your goals, with your personality or if something just "makes sense," don't reinvent the wheel – just become an affiliate and market it to your list of contacts!

Some things you should consider when about whether or not to become an affiliate of a particular product, are:

How does this product benefit you in growing your business?

Does this product appear to have a great earning potential?

Is this a product that is easy for other people to understand?

      Easy to grasp the concept.

      Easily understood compensation plan.

      Done-For-You Marketing Plan / Materials.

      Affordable Entry Point/Fees:

          - Moderate price entry point.

          - No additional significant monthly expenses.

              - Automated commission structures.

      Is this a product that has recurring uses for end clients (not a one-time use)?

      Is this a product that has recurring commissions for you?

      Is this a product with unlimited growth potential?

          - Continuous earnings / growth opportunity.

          - Continuous improvements to the product/services.

          - Continuous training / encouragement for marketers.

      Is there a dedicated customer support staff to

handle issues?
> - So you do not have to learn customer
> support issues for this product.
> - The company handles all end user support.
> - "24-7" support (if possible).

What Should You Do If You Don't Know What to Do?

But what happens if you cannot find an acceptable program that meets the needs of your end user in the way that you want to help them?

Well, that is where you might want to consider creating your own product and offering it for sale. Not only will you be able to meet the needs of your "avatar clients," but you will also catch the attention of other marketers who may help you in selling to their lists also. That will give you an expanded list of clients! And increase your income!

In other words, YOU will become the creator and YOU will hire other affiliates to sell YOUR program! In order to effectively do that, you will need to develop your own training program (and make sure it is a high quality program).

The last section of this book will explain a few steps in that process...

But for right now, let's look at getting your income stream started quickly! The fastest way to accomplish that is to use affiliate marketing. This will be the fastest and the easiest way for you to accomplish your initial goal of making some additional income, build your list and build your online business!

Where Can You Find Quality Affiliate Marketing Opportunities?

You can do your research online. You can Google *"affiliate marketing opportunities"* and you will see more than 62 million results! *(Have fun weeding through all of that)!*

If you do not want to go through 62 million websites to see what they have - there has to be a better way.

Of course, the best way is "Word of Mouth!" **A referral.** That's right!

Think about it...

If you need to hire a plumber or electrician to help with a project around the house, don't you ask your friends for recommendations? People they have used and would use again? Do you take their recommendation in a positive or a negative light?

Positive! Right?

So, if you are looking at getting involved in Affiliate Marketing, why not seek out someone who has had a positive experience with an affiliate product? Their recommendation will guide you to what they have had success with. It will still be up to YOU to decide if this matches with your personality and your goals.

As I said before, if it does not match up with what you are looking for, you are under no obligation to sign up! But if it does match up with your goals and your personality, and it was highly recommended by someone you trust – **GO FOR IT!**

There are also a few websites that deal in affiliate marketing products. They act as a "clearing house" of sorts. "Click Bank" is one such site. "JV Zoo" is another. "Warrior Plus" is a third. And there are many others that are not as well known.

But, as with most sites that deal in affiliate marketing products, there will be good products and there will be some that are not so good. It is up to you to learn each websites rating system and try to make a determination on whether or not a particular product will fit your personality, style and goals.

In that light (of giving recommendations), I would be negligent if I did not provide you with a link to an affiliate marketing opportunity that has taken off like gang busters and is making tremendous impact in North America right now.

A Quick Affiliate Recommendation

The basic concept is "giving away" a **Cash Back App** that is used by people in normal, everyday shopping at normal, everyday stores. A person does not have to purchase lotions, vitamins or products that they really do not want. They simply go to a restaurant (IHOP; Longhorn, etc.) or go to a store (Macy's, JC Penny, etc.) or go and buy pet food and supplies (Petco), just like they normally would do.

But, when they check out, instead of handing the clerk their credit or debit card, they go to the app, purchase an

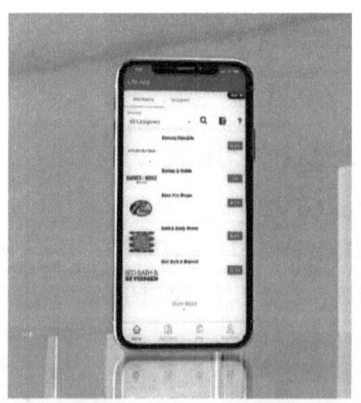 "e-gift card" for the exact amount (using their credit or debit card anyway), and then turn their phone around and allow the clerk to scan gift card from the phone! DONE!

Here is a link to a video that explains how the app works!

http://bit.ly/cashbackappvideo

Let me tell you how it has worked for me. In my first 33 days of using the app, I earned ALMOST $75 in cash back! Just in normal, everyday shopping that we do on a monthly basis! I had 27 purchases in those 33 days.

Dashboard

Welcome, Robert Thibodeau

Dashboard
Profile
Favorites
Wallet
Order History

Available Cash   Redeem Cash   **$74.71**

Lifetime Cash Earned $74.71

If I can do that, in just my first month without doing anything extra – imagine what you could do!

Imagine what it could do for those you share it with!

There are over 250 companies that take the app and provide cash back. Anywhere from 1% up to 20% cash back. Over 450,000 locations in North America! I've never seen anything like this!

And YOU get paid by the company for sharing the app!

You share the app with someone. They use the app. You receive a percentage of the amount THEY spend!

If you want to become a team leader and earn even more, then there is a higher Affiliate Opportunity that has higher earnings potential (and it is possible to earn significant income, just from "sharing the app" and telling your story (like I just did)!

How Does This Become An Affiliate Marketing Opportunity?

This opportunity is awesome! It is so easy. It is so clear. It is so beneficial as you help others achieve their goals!

I am not going to type out everything I truly need to tell you. Why?

Because it has already been explained in video and written formats for us by the company! (Remember, when I stated earlier, *"Don't reinvent the wheel")?*

There are so many benefits to this Affiliate Marketing program, I really can't explain them all here in this book.

I have put a link to my website down below. The reason I'm not going to put a link directly to the **Cash Back App or the Affiliate Marketing** information is simple. This information is constantly being updated as more and more stores and restaurants are coming on board. And more benefits are being added all of the time (like GroupOn is now on the app. BitCoin is coming through the app in the summer of 2019).

From time to time, the links may be changed by the company. So instead of having to edit and republish this book, I will put the links to the company programs on a dedicated page on my website.

Then I will only have to update the links on that page and whoever is reading this book will have the correct link!

Does that sound good? Great!

Here is the link that will provide you with more information on what is quickly becoming one of the most popular and profitable affiliate marketing programs to come along in a very long time! http://rthibodeau.com/cashapp/cash-back-app-affiliate-opportunity/

(If you are reading this online, you should be able to click the link above or copy and paste in your URL. If you are reading the physical copy of this book, please type out the link in your URL to be taken directly to the page).

Finally, for those that may be interested in creating your own Affiliate Marketing product and having others sell that product for you, I will conclude with some basic information that will point you down the correct path.

Developing Your Own Training Program

The following are the types of questions you should answer as you develop your own Affiliate Program. Not only will you be able to help your ideal clients, but you should be able to help other marketers as well. This will help them to help their clients, while generating revenue for you as well.

How does this product help YOU, as the marketer, to help your ideal client?

It must be a product that has benefits the intended client can use. If the ultimate end user cannot use the services you are offering, they will not buy out of need. Most likely, they will be "convinced" to try the product (using the "money back guarantee" if they do not see the results). That is not what you want!

You want a product that is easy for the client to use. You do not want to create something that has multiple steps that will take a lot of time to figure out. You must grab the end user's attention and get them results fast – or they will cancel on you.

I once bought a 93-part video course on some aspect of Internet Marketing (it was several years ago). The pitch was *"we covered every aspect you could think of."* I thought that would be great! Everything in one place.

Each video was only about 15 minutes long. I watched the first dozen or so videos over a few days. It took something like 4 hours of my time and I was even more confused than when I began. I still have them somewhere on my computer or server. But I've never gone back to them.

Bottom line: Don't over complicate things for the end user OR the marketers who will be selling your product!

You must have a product that is not expensive for the client to use. There also needs to be enough of a profit for the marketers who will help you sell to the end users. Otherwise, they will not want to take *their* time to market *your* product.

But, at the same time, you cannot just "mark up" your product unnecessarily for the end user. They are going to evaluate their need and your claim to be able to meet that need. They will then compare that to the price you are asking. They will be asking themselves, "Is it worth it?" (in their mind) whether or not they should make the investment.

That needs to be the determining factor. Do not simply price something in an effort to gain marketers to sell the product to their lists. You need to price it according to the need it will fulfill for the end user.

Sell The Destination – Not the Journey!

You need to sell the "destination" and not "the journey."

For example: If I am selling you a vacation to Hawaii, I want to tell you all about the great time you will have **THERE.** I am going to tell you about the tours and the exotic food and the blue ocean and great accommodations. I'm going to focus on all of the things you will do and price it accordingly. I am **NOT** going to tell you about the 8-hour flight or about the two layovers of two hours each. I am **NOT** going to tell you to be at the airport two hours before your flight for the security check-in line. I am **NOT** going to tell you it will cost $10 per day to park your car. I am **NOT** going to tell you to bring air sickness medicine. That is *"the journey."*

I am only going to focus on the *"Destination"* in order to sell you the trip! Not the journey!

As you design this training, you need to make sure you are able to "sell the destination" to the end user. This will help other affiliate marketers to sell more of the product for you as well.

Robert Thibodeau

What Should You Do Now?

Well, if you are interested in generating an additional stream of income that will not be dependent upon your current job (so if you were to lose your job and the income from the job, you would not lose the additional stream of income), then affiliate marketing is probably the right choice for you!

You can do the research yourself (over 62 million affiliate marketing opportunities are on Google - right now) ...

You can go to the major affiliate marketing websites and sort through the thousands of different affiliate marketing opportunities listed on those sites...

One Word of Warning

BEWARE of all the claims of thousands and thousands of dollars of income right off the bat! Some marketers will show you "their PayPal accounts" (or some other such thing) trying to prove to you their system works. It may – or it may not.

One thing they do not show you from the "sales in their PayPal account," is all of the expenses they paid to get those results.

Let's assume a $10,000 balance in sales is showing in their PayPal account. Take into account about ½ of that is going to go towards advertising (Facebook Ads, etc.). Another 1/3 is going to be paid to other marketers who are selling that product on the Affiliate system.

So, out of the $10K showing, "maybe" the person doing the video will show a profit of $3000. That is still "not bad" for income. And if a person could do that on a weekly basis, it would be great!

But DO NOT fall for that gimmick of "let me show you my PayPal account and you can see the amount of sales I made."

THIS IS A BUSINESS! Do not ever forget that!

If you had a traditional "brick and mortar" business, you would have rent, utilities, employee salaries, stock to buy, and advertising costs. So a $100K per month income might only net you $10K in profits.

Online marketing, and especially developing and then using Affiliate Marketing to sell your own product is going to be the same way.

Remember this as well. You do not want to invest in something that requires you to buy products you do not really want to use. If you don't want to use the lotions, vitamins, laundry soap, etc., neither will many of the other people you talk to. And if the only reason you continue to order them is so you can get a commission on what others are buying (and remember, they don't really want to use them either), it will not be long before your commissions will cease.

I can truly say, that every single time I fell for those claims, I also FAILED in my Affiliate Marketing attempt using their product. Was it me? Or was it just a bad product? Or a bad marketing program?

Also remember, if it is "easy" to get a lot of money quickly, it will also be "easy" for it to go away just as quickly! You need to make sure the money will come in, but consistently. It should always be steadily increasing. It should allow you to be the one in control of how much and how fast you make the additional income (not someone else).

You can also ask for recommendations from someone you trust. Someone who has been "around the block" a few times. Someone who has been burned a few times along the way. Someone who has learned a lot of lessons concerning what constitutes a "good" program versus a "bad" program.

I hope the information I have put together for you has provided you with some level of confidence that I am a person who fits that criteria. I want you to notice that I am NOT showing you all the income I've received, etc. in an effort to *convince* you to join this program. That is not my intent and I intentionally did not go down that road.

IF you decide to join, I want it to be for one reason only – you did the research and decided this fits your personality and your goals. Period!

I did explain my success with the Cash Back App just to show you that it really does work! You can GIVE AWAY this app and it will bless those who use it! There is no requirement they (or you) join the affiliate program in order to use the app! They (and you) can have the app for FREE! That is why I explained a little bit about my success with the Cash Back App earlier.

Concerning the affiliate marketing opportunity – I want YOU to go to the link (which will take to the page on my website containing the most up-to-date links for the information you need about the program) and check it out for yourself.

If you have ANY questions, you can reach out to me through the contact form on my website and I will get back to you.

Go to this link on my website
http://rthibodeau.com/cashapp/cash-back-app-affiliate-opportunity/
(where you will find the links to the video's that explain how the cash back app works and how to get the app and also the links for the information on the Affiliate Marketing Program).

Happy Selling and Have a Blessed Future in this new business venture you are starting!

Robert Thibodeau

For more information on other products, services or to get in touch with Robert Thibodeau, please visit our website at www.bobthibodeau.com

Robert Thibodeau

Other Books By Robert Thibodeau

How One Cup of Coffee Can Change Your World -

https://amzn.to/2HslgeN

Blind Faith: How to Receive What You Cannot See -

https://amzn.to/2EjsEHs

7 Keys to Answered Prayer -

https://amzn.to/2Ejvmwm

The Six Trials of Jesus – https://amzn.to/2QeKIHp

www.ingramcontent.com/pod-product-compliance
Lightning Source LLC
Chambersburg PA
CBHW030736180526
45157CB00008BA/3188